AF215987

Tim Cumming

Contact Print

Wrecking Ball Press

© Tim Cumming

Contact Print

First Edition

Cover Design Owen Benwell

Published in 2002 by
Wrecking Ball Press
9 Westgate • North Cave • Brough • East Yorkshire • HU15 2NG

The junior government minister,
also big in plastics,
disconnects his microphone
and is led from the outside broadcast vehicle
to the ministerial car
and as the car drives away
he unwraps a pastry from a paper serviette
and eats it, cupping
his hand under his mouth
until the car reaches
a set of traffic lights
and a panhandler with a rag and bucket
steps out to wipe the windscreen.
As the lights change to amber
he steps to the driver's window
and knocks on the glass.
The minister leans forward
to speak to the driver
as the car inches forward with the traffic
and without turning the driver
unlocks the rear door
and the panhandler jumps in,
smothering the minister's face with the rag,
and the car drives off at speed.

Six months later
it's summertime, and used office
furniture has spread across
both sides of the street
with the sprawl you see
in a Spring tide,
in drinkers at a bar.

A camera in a nearby supermarket
takes a photograph,
for this is a street
where you see pictures snap
to a frame where ever you look.
Not because things happen here
though sometimes they do;
the money falls short, people vanish,
things get weird. A funeral march plays,
which boy kicked the football over the hearse?
A car rolls three times then settles.
The minister's body was found near here.

The story of his life flaps on a theatre bill.
A little girl tears it from a post,

runs across the road and falls over.
She gets up and carries on running
but she's captured in this picture nonetheless.
For several minutes there's no escaping it.

The men who spend their day on the street
between stacked furniture, tables and desks,
watch the traffic's progress
and stretch their legs
across the pavement,
leaning on the backs of their chairs

with the sprung poise
of soldiers at ease.
One of them has a face like burnt plastic.

Two blocks back men are laying tar
and someone knocks a stone from their shoe
as Tony Harris, his name
on his card and on his lover's lips
beats a drummer's voodoo
on the dashboard of a stationary Ford
and picks a piece of food
from the collar of his jacket
whose cut is like
a tidemark from the 1970s.
He wore it to a party
where he first met Stella.
She looked him in the eye.
'For some reason,' she said, 'I'm with him,'
and gestured to her husband.
All evening he was under surveillance.
They kissed once, by the downstairs toilets.

They'll spend the afternoon together.
He's late though, stuck in traffic
stretching from Highbury corner
to the cinema where the bottleneck
of a demonstration
spills out over the green
into the Essex Road, the Angel,
like page upon page of illegible handwriting.

The atmosphere's calm, there's music, slogans.
It's summer. Police sit in windowless vans,
a helicopter circles overhead
like something from a Greek myth.
A police horse pushes people back against
the railings on the green
and that could be a myth as well.

Cyclists zigzag between the marchers and the traffic.

Some drivers have left their cars
to take the sun or make a stand,
to stand and look,
but Tony sees a man in black in the back
of some one else's garden
smoking a cigarette. His dead brother Michael sits
in a dark corner of his head
wearing a polo shirt with anchors on each collar
waving a piece of paper
with dance steps on it.

One thing always leads to another.

10

Tony Harris, this is your life.
It feels like anything could happen.
A man runs out of a building shouting *fire!*
Another kicks the chair from his legs
and hangs like a chandelier.

There's a knock at the door, your father's voice,
Mozart on original instruments,
the sound of the crowd, a roadworks drill.
Your first words
on a graph that measures explosions,
earthquakes, the seas of the moon
on the side we don't see,
shells in our pockets.
Tony, you've been there,
you've been in love.
The weight of the world subtracts from you.
You've asked someone to stay and they do
as if you have denied the laws of science.

You've seen your hopes go up in smoke,
struggling in the undergrowth of your signature.
Sometimes you feel like a fold in a piece of paper,
with a picture of you on it,
one you fold close to the bone.

You fold it again and push it into your pocket,
pushing through a frosted glass door
that flushes red in the rear light
of a car reversing into it,

and here you sit in motionless traffic,
your eyes the colour of printer's ink.
They have seen the tide turn
at a depth of ten thousand metres,
and you have turned
on the tide of women's laughter,
from your father's voice on the cellar steps.

You think you have your father's feet,
your mother's eyes,
the way she smiled when drinking,
but what's in between's your own.

Now you're in the driver's seat
brandishing a pair of elementary compasses
and a sense of direction
that's not much larger than a surgical instrument.

A helicopter circles overhead.
You sit in late lunch traffic
on the streets of the outside broadcast.
A security camera takes another picture.

Reader, come closer, pull the curtains to.
We're at Paddington station looking at the notice board
for train departures; looking carefully.
Our movements are essentially those
of anyone whose photograph is taken by ceiling cameras
45 times every minute.
You borrow 20p
and go down to the toilets,
choose the end cubicle and remove your coat,
put down the toilet seat,
take out your wallet, and from the wallet
a single piece of tissue.
Inside the tissue there's a paper wrap
and two pieces of kitchen foil.
One you roll into a tube and kink it,
and you place the other on the toilet cistern.
You put the tube into your mouth
and unfold the paper; in the centre crease
there's what's left of a ten bag
and you knock half of what's left
onto the foil. You open a book of matches,
flush the toilet, strike a match
and hold the flame under the foil.
The drug runs and boils dark brown, then black.
You swallow the smoke and keep it down
maybe twenty seconds
then breathe out slowly, retch, breathe in.
You do this three times.
The effect is immediate, and heightened
by the situation you're in: the toilet, the station, and so on.
Your mouth fills with saliva,
and you lean over the bowl to spit, then straighten,
folding the paper wrap and foil into the tissue paper,
and the tissue back into your wallet.

You count your money, put on your coat
and light a cigarette to hide the smell.
The cigarette tastes good.
You leave the cubicle and wash your hands,
then look in the mirror to check for stains on the teeth.
The toilet attendant looks at you strangely as you leave
because you're smoking
and also because the attendant looks at everyone
in exactly this way.
But the look unnerves you.
You take the steps three at a time
and walk back into the station
where Tony's dead brother Michael is waiting,
in black as usual,
noting you have taken just over ten minutes.

The finger of government barely touches here,
stopping at a worn tyre, a head of hair,
or tapping the glasses in the bar across the road,
the clicking sound of *tax, tax, taxi,*
skimming the cream off the milk delivered
to the Indian shops, the supermarket open till midnight,
where a shop assistant stacks butter pads into a
refrigerator
then walks to the front door where his figure's reflected
in the curved and tinted windows of the undertakers
where he sees the head of the demonstration.

A green cleaning bucket's on the floor beside him
and above a plane at 36,000 feet crosses another,
whose vapour trail the wind distracts,
and finds itself reflected in this bucket.

No one, nothing here leaves much behind it.

Tony, you could be struggling between two men
in the doorway of a snooker hall
and never be seen again
and who would know
or think it worth a picture
and if a picture were taken
mark an ex where the ball should be?

Tony's hand goes to his wallet,
fumbling the way he fumbled with girls.
You want to show us something, your wedding picture?
Your confirmation medal?
Are you choking,
is that wheat swaying in a childhood flashback?

The day they found your dead brother Michael
was the day of the terrorist outrage.
You got into your car and put on the radio.
The news that the gunmen laughed like hyenas
disturbs you because you have laughed like a hyena,
your hands buried in women's hair
where ideas were taking shape
and hang the consequences
which ran like milk or wire mesh through glass
if glass, its properties, could be said
to be a metaphor of what you were capable of
rather than what you did,
but people did terrible things, Tony.

You've turned to someone, looked them in the eye.
You've shown them your teeth.
You know them by their weight.
Λ photograph was taken of the body on the steps.

Tony sits in frozen traffic
and punches a tape into the machine.

A voice starts talking about
The Feeling of Feeling.
Traffic is blocked in both directions

as lunchtime drinkers
leave the Tappet Hen
blinking at the open door
and stalling to ignite cigarettes,

eyes like whiskey chasers,
a contact print of silhouettes.

At the top of a winding staircase
a man stands with his eyes closed.
A woman comes to in an unlit room.
You've known that man, that woman's voice.
Someone makes a speech on a box.
A boxer beats a punchball
while another stabs a map on a wall
and says something true about Tony
like *he was half the price his father was*

and time was it would've mattered
but Tony sees a different picture,
something to shake with both hands.

He grinds to a stop two streets from his destination
and tries on a smile for size
taken from one of the Borgia Popes;
it fits like a rubber glove.
Grabs a bunch of cut iris wrapped in a racing page
(his second-runner *Party Politics*)
and a sheet of home news;
woman bursts into flames outside hostel;
man loses crown during foreplay;
the Prime Minister's heart weighs 2 1/4 ounces.

A panhandler weaves in and out of the traffic
with a rag and bucket. Grimacing into the mirror
Tony sees the cars behind, and the crowd.
A door slams on a truck.
Some one starts dancing outside a fish shop.
In an endless loop where his mind takes him
he saw Stella uncouple the straps of her dress

and it felt as if their lives had been
laid down like track to where they lay
and where they put their hands.

The car parked slanting into the kerb
by the refurbished George with its canary yellow paintwork,
satellite sport booming on the far wall,
he makes his way to Stella's front door,
a blue door with frosted glass.
She looks troubled as her arms enfold him.
They have the afternoon,
and they kiss, make drinks and talk,
about the past, mostly.
Her husband's name comes up three times
like a suicide in a country and western song,
but Tony felt he'd never existed in the way a really good
country and western song existed.
She wants to leave her husband again.
Tony's face hardens like gum.
He pulls her to him and cradles her head
to his chest like a telephone
She's crying, and when she has stopped crying
she leaves the room saying, "I can't go out.
My eyes are swollen."

Instead, she sways down the hall to shower,
and left alone, Tony considers the future
which looks like the past, but wider, all horizon.
Who knows what to do about tomorrow?
It simply appears like dampness or heat,
a picture window of opportunity.

From the kitchen the sound of a kettle on.
He fills the armchair like a small god
and steam slowly fills the room. Later he makes coffee
and pads up stairs behind Stella to the bedroom,
working his Barry White impression.
They've known each other a year, more or less,
and he wants to tell her what he feels, exactly,
but something gets lost in translation,
the tense and gender are wrong.

He looks at her as if looking for the right word,
but reader, he stops before he starts,
the curtains drop.

Stella climbs into bed beside him.
The phone rings three times then stops.
"That was you-know-who," she says,
nodding towards her wedding picture

and turning the dimmers low
she twists out of her black underwear
as Tony crouches over her,
stroking her back with the same movements
that someone makes cleaning a window
or wiping a mirror.

She checks the clock on the bedside table
then turns to him
as if turning a screw through the dead centre
of his heart, pushing him back onto the mattress

and sticking her tongue in his mouth.
Her tongue bobs like a cork on water.

And still that persistent buzzing
the lorryload of hot tar
on the corner of the public library
and holes being dug all over the city.
What were they looking for? What was lost?
Sunlight glinting on the body of a Dutch jet
heading west for Greenland, Canada
and the Eastern seaboard, *Time Cop* on video
and Tony's overnight bag on the carousel.

Then it must be New York, Chicago,
Kansas, Texas and south to Mexico
and a second nightfall of the day
in which the rains have come
and streets are filled with too many soldiers.
They look bored and they are,
leaning on their semi automatics.

Here in the south of continuous consonants
the market by the church is busy
and all the buses full,
and this the time of one ox, one horse,
one crop, one chicken in the yard,
and one bullet, one chance only
and one truck, two blades,
the dogs in the yard,
a letter in an envelope of hair,
the broken down bus from Tluxcla
and sometimes gunfire
and sometimes an election broadcast.

The names of the towns, their streets, their senators
spread out across the map
like exotic dishes on a menu.
People turn in their sleep
in Texas, in Vancouver,
a computer programmer sips decaf in Seattle,
a potter plans a window display
in a bus station in Santa Ana,
a priest visiting Grace Cathedral in San Francisco
has a wet dream and rolls over it,
Frankie and Johnnie and Conway Twitty
shiver while pissing in a toilet
as a black cleaner pushes a mop into the stalls.

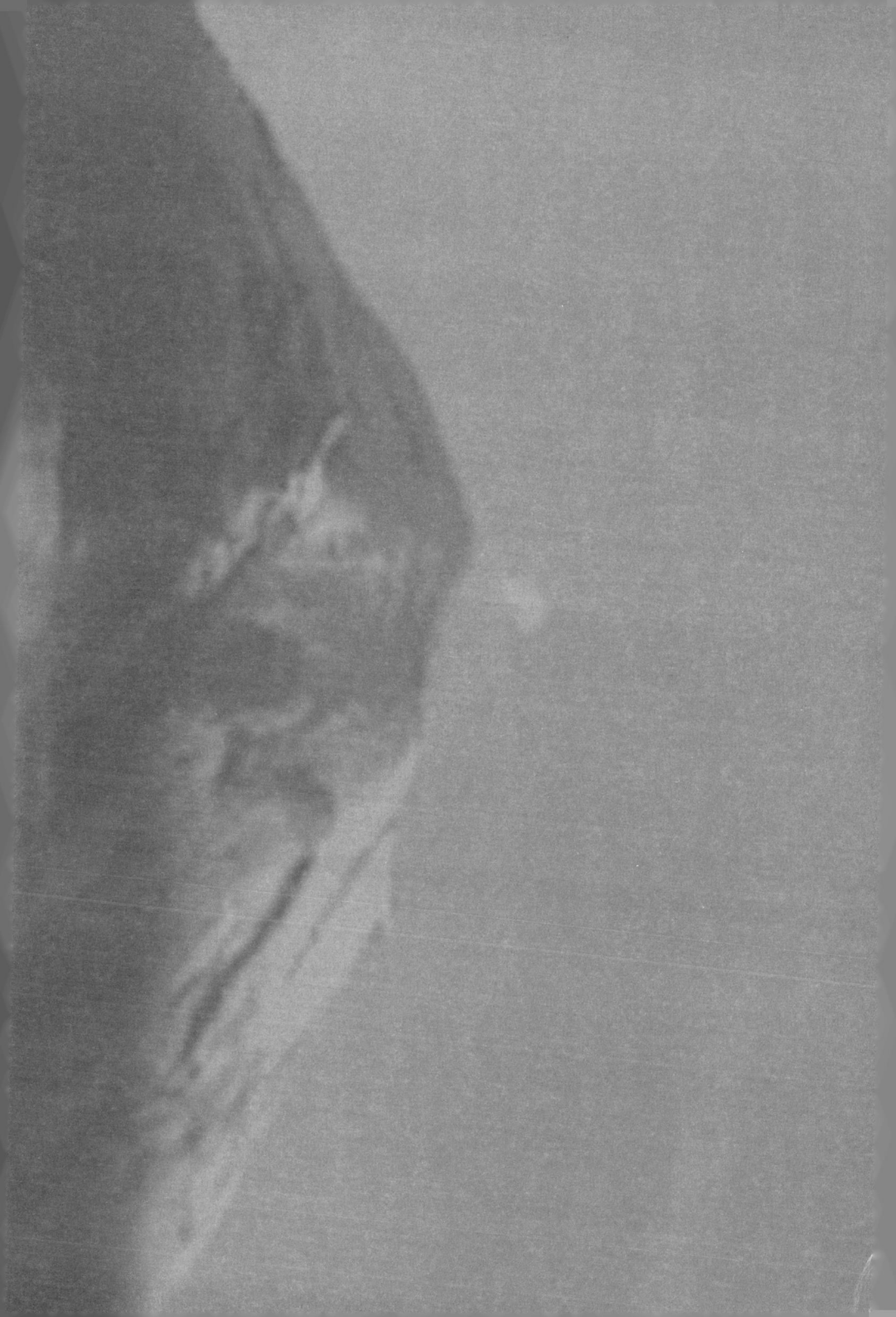

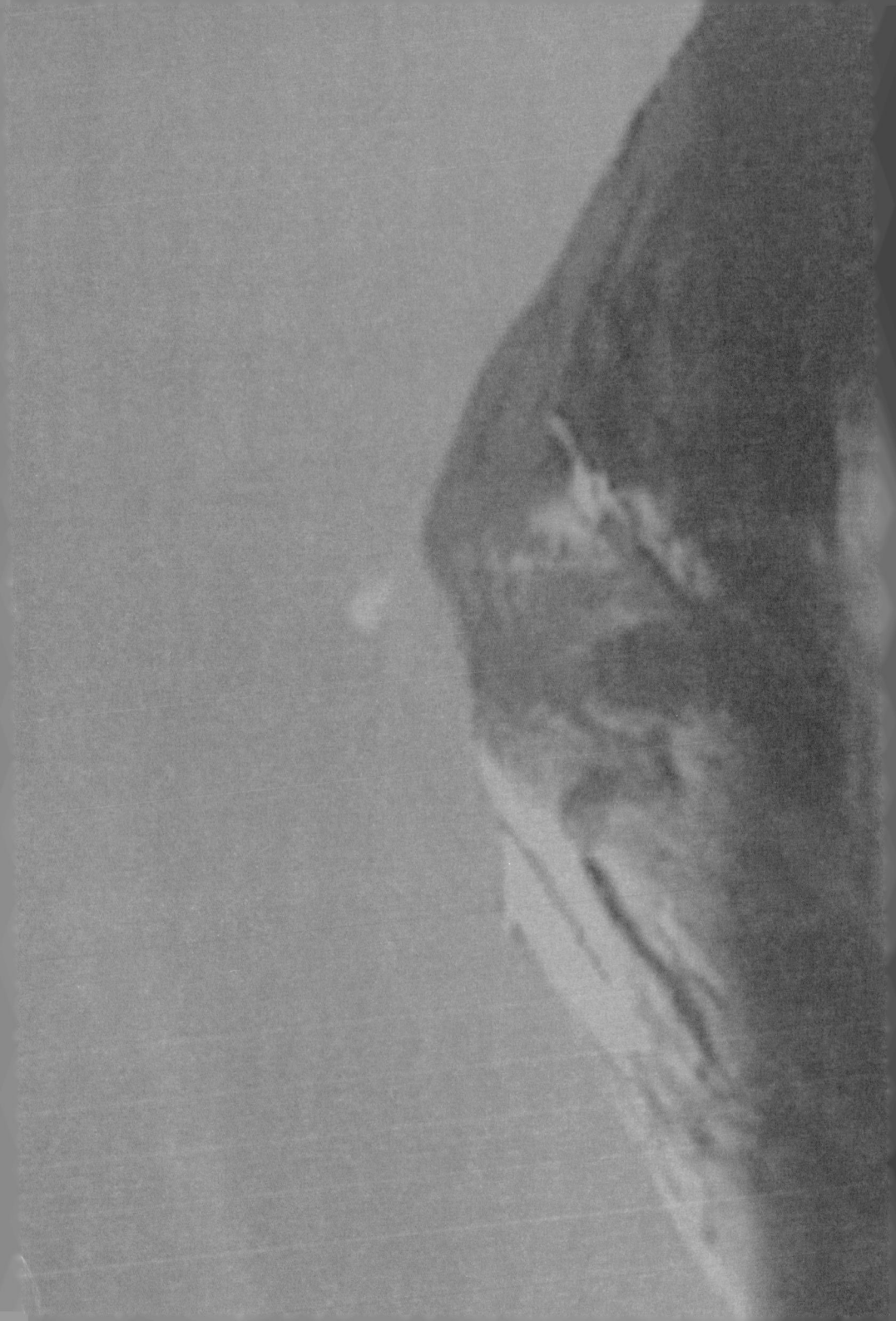

A couple of Swedish businessmen shoot pool
in a Mexico City pool hall.
A gun goes off in an Indian cantina

and a house stands empty with all lights blazing
in a café owner's memory of childhood.
Cattle roam all over Texas and Argentina,
Japanese tour groups spend millions in Vegas
while Frankie eats eggs and beans
with a Puerto Rican prostitute named Margarita, 21,
a waitress at Caesar's Palace,
talking about her two-year-old son in her mother's home in
Miami.

Breakers crashed onto the white sands
of an empty beach on the Pacific coast
as a man crushes his hat in his hands in Ocosingo
shouting he'd been robbed.
Women walk barefoot in the restaurant kitchens
of a three-star hotel named after a president,
the maitre 'd clipping his toenails
in the pantry, one foot resting on a meat hook,
the other stubbed against the spine
of Richard Burton's *Kama Sutra*.
All the best books get their spines broken.

And the company president's only boy
who befriended all the dogs in the valley,
even the lame,
especially the lame.

How a man watching a plane taxi onto the runway
thought of his dead wife,
his girlfriend in Vera Cruz
and what she was doing there, and how.

A gardener tended
a garden of box and palm dug around
an unfinished, now abandoned concrete villa

as a saxophone player
with skin the colour of dust
played phrases on the pavement in front of the Café Colonial.
A thin man walked with a gut string guitar past the tables,
how four of them were full, three empty,
the television playing in the bar inside the café
and no one watching it,
the cleaner asleep by the unisex toilets,
the smell of dettol in the air,
the sound a someone weeping in a theatre.

Soldiers raised a flag in a park
and saw things that weren't there
and Tony isn't really there
or where he should be,
heat-sealed on his company's headed paper,
but drowning under an aquarium
in a green lit bar,
his face pressed to the glass beside him
and looking
into deep water.

Water is the element of the heart.
Prone to acid flashbacks,
someone who looked like Tony
pushed against a door and opened it,
tripped on the pavement, fell,
sent a sheaf of papers flapping across the road
and Tony, you saw him fall
later that day,
loosened your tie,
thought about Stella,
feeling the edge of things grow thicker,
thought you saw your ex-wife
in the window of a supermarket,
and what you didn't know
you could write on the whites of her eyes.

You left Stella sleeping,
turning in bed to shed
another skin.
You wonder which world she's in,
the weather there.
She drags and holds
like a ship's anchor.
The first time you slept together
she kissed you where it hurts.

They were like two lines meeting on a map.
They both had the same address on their envelopes.
She held up her hands
to show him they were her hands,
as if to say *danger*
If I start now I won't be able to stop.

32

She can still feel the weight of him,
her fingers dug into the grain of his skin,
He sees her sitting at the end of a bed
in a motel bedroom
counting her bruises.
She pulls up her knickers
and talks under her breath.
Her husband's in the bathroom working the mirrors,
taking pictures.
There's bandages on his hands
and the lean, hungry look of persistence.

Stella's husband
knew about Tony.
He'd trailed them once,
walking on his instep.
He'd seen photographs.
He only drank bottled water.

When Stella saw Tony she saw
the cupboard full of the same cotton suit,
the way he chewed on one side
of the mouth when laughing,
See, you're doing it now.
What do you find so funny, Tony?
Your allergy to tomatoes?
The story about the chocolate?

She's behind you, Tony, unbuttoning your shirt,
your stomach falling over the elastic
of your underpants,
the scar on your flank
in the shape of a question mark.

He smooths his hair, present tense,
pushing through the crowd of himself,
Stella spread like dough
on Tony's kitchen table,
the loop of his loose belt
knocking at the side of her knee.
Now he combs his hair across the crown
and works slowly on nicotine gum,
turning the wheel to full lock
and turning like the hands of a clock
against the image of his smoke-filled father

rising up from Stella's bath,
laughing the way he laughed when drinking,
the way Tony liked him best

though aware of a persistent buzzing,
some kind of reminder
but of what – parking up
he shakes his head and rolls in his seat
as if he were riding a horse
from one movie to the next,
the end of the trail
stretching out across mile-wide beaches
the colour of Stella's suntan.

Look closely. What do you see?
Helicopters in formation,
a row of pizza delivery bikes,
schoolboys high on ether.

The demonstration moves east.
A drinker beats his chest with his fist
while talking about nationhood
and someone casts the first stone,
the first punch is thrown.
A hand in a bar shoots up
to beckon a friend in,
someone leans on a snooker cue
and talks loudly about women.
On the other side of the street
two cats lie on the window sill of the Paradise cafe
like a couple of deflated tyres.
There's a brass bed in the flat above,
and the ticking of a clock on the shelf above that
is the tapping of a blind man's cane
through a town square at midnight
in a film of that name,

and he's seen it, Tony has,
counted the steps
from the front door to the back
and still that persistent buzzing,
the circling of a helicopter,

as a busker with skin the colour of old money
played Buddy Holly's *Love is Strange* on the pavement
in front of the public library,
the television above the till inside the cafe
and no one watching it,
the cleaner asleep by the unisex toilets,
the smell of dettol in the air,
the sound of someone sweeping in a theatre
one hand dangling in a jungle pool far from here,

and there goes Tony Harris,
heatsealed in his seventies jacket,
zigzagging up the road, chasing his own satellite.

Skipper it ain't funny how some people
are last seen at a bank
stuffing paper into a bag,
rummaging at the boot of a taxi
a mile from the airport
or leaning over the prow
on the ferry to Bilbao
their clothes neatly folded
and topped with shoes,
the kind of shoes you get hopelessly lost in.

Have you ever been to Bilbao Tony?
Is it true you sit in airports
watching the planes rise?
Do you like to watch, to be watched?

You find a bar to ponder this in,
the pool room of the Queen Victoria,
setting up a game
and clearing the table in one lucky break.

What made you tick resembled a tangle of brambles in
a thicket.
You drained your glass
and called for another,
thought you saw your ex-wife with Stella, her
husband,

and a fourth, a stranger, your brother
laughing in a huddled group
in a second-hand furniture shop across the street,
around a piano which played
ghostly tunes by itself.

There was the sound of the chamber of a gun being turned

and Tony, you wiped that smile of yours
and lay belly up and in a position
suspiciously post-coital,
at the southernmost tip of your imagination

coiled under the lid of your mother's bureau of jewels, a
necklace

at whose clasp you used to prosper;
taking it, breaking it
and watching the glass beads tumble and roll
into dangerous places

and you can read here your future
if not your palm
or the swing of the club
on the course after business,
the kind of business that ends in a killing.
Then the wicker basket of dried flowers
in the hall of Stella's house,
a man's umbrella loose in the stand,
a pair of weights on the living room floor.

You push through a glass door
with your name on it
noticing your footprints are getting smaller,
there's a shallow depression
at the top of the stairs
of the first house you remember,

your father turning like a screw at the door
of his room, walking down the landing
towelling himself into middle age,
a kind of perpetual seven-o-clock
slouch in his gait,

the big skeletal hand raised toward noon and `halleluluah'
your brother Michael pyjama'd at the top step,
pricking his feet with a needle, his sink full of bottles.
He's shaking your shoulder, Tony,
saying things that haven't been said in years.
He loves you, Tony,
his knees buckled around his waist
in an attitude many once mistook for adolescent promise.

There is the family home,
and there your neighbour,
her father's Reliant askew in the drive,
her mother at the end of her tether,
her reasons for leaving
in full, in triplicate, inebriate.

A light goes on in an upstairs room
at a picture window
at which Tony, your face peers moonward,
mournful.

Your first wife stands behind you.
You slap her twice, hard.

You glance at your watch,
look around for a chemist,
find an off-licence,
buy a Bells in a brown bag.
A sewing machine rattles across the past.
You see two people coming and going
in a room you half-recognise,
a woman you half-understood
grinding her teeth for what seems days
mumbling instructions, plans, settlements.

She said, *what am I to you?*
When will I see you?
What do you see in me?
He thought how good it would be
if people could evaporate.

Is it force of habit
or force of nature
that makes us do the things we do?
We'll never here the end of the bass line in that question, Tony.
That rise in the tone of your voice defines you.

A young boy walks into your head,
takes down his trousers, fiddles with himself.

You're with your father walking down a street
and through a door you half-recognise into a room
of bedroom furniture large enough to stand under.

It's dark inside, Stella's lying back in your mother's cream gown
smoking a cigarette on your mother's bed
and you can hear your father's tread on the stairs.

You think there are 26 steps,
one for every letter of the alphabet
which is far back as you remember.
Beyond that is programmer's code,
painting by binary numbers

and for a moment you're stuck
among the zeroes and ones
moving under your skin,
you can see your dead brother Michael rise
in the dark of a motel bathroom

and from there to here through a long tunnel
in the highroad static

he comes running down the hallway.
He has something to tell you, a warning,
and you kill the engine,

stalling over Stella's shoulder,
at your parents' bedroom door,
at the hands on the clock
above the second bed
that mother bought the year
your voice broke
at which point the door cracks
and you turn, startled,
spilling your drink
then turning back
to the needle
of a speedometer
which is reading zero,

as crowds from the demonstration
part into the traffic of the capital.

This movement you're in's
more subtle than sunset.

You shift in your seat,
reaching for a cigarette,
loosely fitting your father's silhouette
which you can still faintly see turning away
at the top of the stairs
in the first house you can remember,
at the window on the landing facing West,
a red moon behind and three yellow sodium lamps
like three Christmas baubles.

Him of the important missing words
the answerphone's speech
the spot the ball commentary.

He knew the steps
and when to sweep the steps from view.
They led upstairs to Stella's bed
and down the other side
to an unlit backstreet in the submerged town
in which the tolling of a bell
was the bell of Tony's dreamless sleep
swinging at the ribs,
ringing from the mouth and chest
with a heart at the centre of it,
and the drumming of fingers, of drummers,
of rain and soldiers in fatigues

and Indian country, border crossings,
the band setting up in some Southern Gothic auditorium
where everyone, everything was much too thin
like thin gruel at a high altitude
and the women had sharp little teeth
and the lower halves of men were made of wax

and somewhere a spine shivered,
a head was shaved,
someone shined a shoe, or filled it,
or lost it along with all their luggage
and their fortune

and Tony narrowed to a single line on an upward spiral,
sipping his drink
thinking what it must've been like
hearing Buddy play and the crickets sing
in the fields behind the auditorium

among the Buicks and pick up trucks,
between the shoe blacks
and in the mouths of the bar attendants
shining glasses and pulling beer
from chrome taps
while *Love is Strange* plays
on the dime of a dime store drinker,
still young, counting what he has in his pocket.

In the air the sound of rolling thunder
and women's laughter.
Oh to be the cause, says Tony,
holding his glass to the window
where the sun slants in
and the barman slopes over steaming new glasses
caught between shade, smoke and heaven
and this is the result,

Tony licking salt from his lips,
sat in front of the serving hatch
where a couple of plates of pub tandoori
steam into the light. Tony she's right;
"I never saw him blink," she said
and you could tell by the look in her eyes
she was looking at stuff
you couldn't see, Tony.
You think of fire and ice,
the life cycle of a comet.

A sea bell tolls a mile from shore
at the mouth of the harbour
all through winter.
I was a child there,
throwing a ball
to the daughter of my neighbour

but this is a line of enquiry you turn from
with a shrug of your shoulders
and sinking down into the upholstery of the bar,
finger a small slit below your knee
revealing frayed fake leather and foam
and the springs beneath.

As your tongue seeks a cavity
the news pops and flashes on the pub TV,
someone takes a photograph
of the first body stretchered from the demonstration,
the bottles, cans and coins thrown
into whatever future finds them,
then as now resisting arrest, as guilty
as gaffer tape, the heart giving out;
it's there in the book like the pills
in the sink, the wrong turn taken,
the road untravelled.
You'll get there, Tony,
dancing out of time,
and time was,
but you're still alive, and orbiting,
you've got to keep moving,
it's the movie you're in.
The voices in your head begin to thicken.
You don't know what to do but you do it,
the improbable course of the hurricane, the comet.
Stiff as a brush a second barman
moves between tables
wiping and shaking ash into a bucket.

Tony momentarily blinks into the sun
as it breaks on his glass,
looks back on things,
weaving with the house spirits,
arranges them in Sistine fashion.

He'd had a few drinks,
pooling to himself like mercury.

The colour of his interior would always be
the colour of his eyes,
a milky lapis lazuli,
the colour of his dreamless sleep.
He saw the gap between what he was
and what he did
and couldn't bridge it.

The sun was much lower,
the shadows deeper.
A skeleton hung in a joke shop window,
the city was spread out
like a set of meccano,

but lonelier, heavier, larger and more beautiful
than he remembered it being,
and he accepted it,
as the realisation clicked
like a shot and then a shout
from a car at the end of the street

and people moved between the traffic
and a little girl ran across the road
and the yellow lights of the fast food stand,
the orange face of the short order cook,
the cough of an engine at his shoulder,
the sound of a door being slammed, a glass door,
the train pulling away from the station
past the listed gasometers, the jagged angles
of the remaining factories, their plant machinery,
the council blocks towering over the public park,
couples lying under each tree ringing the "happiness" bell,
a boy kicking a football across the green,
the sudden panorama of the city and its spaces
repeating itself to the horizon.